The Hidden Value in Your
Life Insurance

Funds for your Retirement

Darwin M. Bayston, CFA, and Daryn N. Teague

abbott press

Abbott Press books may be ordered through booksellers or by contacting:

Abbott Press
1663 Liberty Drive
Bloomington, IN 47403
www.abbottpress.com
Phone: 1 (866) 697-5310

Because of the dynamic nature of the Internet, any web addresses or links contained in this book may have changed since publication and may no longer be valid. The views expressed in this work are solely those of the author and do not necessarily reflect the views of the publisher, and the publisher hereby disclaims any responsibility for them.

Any people depicted in stock imagery provided by Thinkstock are models, and such images are being used for illustrative purposes only.
Certain stock imagery © Thinkstock.

ISBN: 978-1-4582-2020-2 (sc)
ISBN: 978-1-4582-2021-9 (e)

Library of Congress Control Number: 2016906581

Print information available on the last page.

Abbott Press rev. date: 6/17/2016

Contents

Disclaimer

This publication is designed to provide information solely about the subject matter covered. It is sold with the understanding that neither the author nor the publisher is engaged by the reader to render legal, financial, investment, accounting, or other professional service. If legal advice or other expert assistance is required by the reader, the services of a competent professional should be sought. The purpose of this book is to educate. Neither the author nor the publisher shall have any liability or responsibility to any person or entity with respect to any loss or damage caused, or alleged to be caused, directly or indirectly, by the information contained in this book.

Circular 230 Disclosure: Pursuant to recently enacted U.S. Treasury Department Regulations, we are now required to advise you that, unless otherwise expressly indicated, any federal tax advice contained in this communication, including attachments and enclosures, is not intended or written to be, and may not be used, for the purpose of (1) avoiding tax-related penalties under the Internal Revenue Code, or (2) promoting, marketing or recommending to another party any tax-related matters addressed herein.

Preface

There is no shortage of books written in response to the retirement savings crisis in America. Many of these books offer all sorts of great advice about financial planning and counsel intended to help Americans adequately fund their retirement.

This is not another one of those books.

This book was written to educate American seniors about the hidden value of their life insurance policies. Our goal is to let you in on the details of a financial planning strategy that many seniors just like you have used to help fund their retirement and improve their quality of life in those precious golden years.

In fact, this strategy is so beneficial to seniors who no longer need or can afford their life insurance policies that many life insurance companies don't want it to be known. Some even prohibit the agent who sold you the policy from telling you about this option.

The authors would not have been able to tell this story in the pages that follow without the assistance of Wesley Costa. Wesley provided valuable editorial input in the development of each chapter, offered important suggestions that improved the quality of the manuscript, and brought to bear his considerable creative skills to help illustrate various elements of the book. We are indebted to him for his contributions to this project.

Introduction

Discovering A Hidden Asset

Jim is an 81 year-old widower in Florida living on a fixed income. He receives a modest check each month from Social Security and has about $120,000 remaining from his hard-earned life savings.

Unfortunately, as a result of the unpredictable ups and downs of the financial markets -- combined with the low interest rates earned on CDs and treasury bonds -- his retirement savings haven't produced the kind of income he had hoped. Meanwhile, Jim's health has begun to decline a bit and he now has some medical issues, resulting in rising bills for doctor visits and the prescription medications he needs every month.

Then one day, Jim collected his mail and came across an unwelcome surprise that rocked his world.

The letter from his life insurance company informed him that, due to unforeseen circumstances that have hurt the company's profitability, they were going to be raising the premiums on Jim's $250,000 universal life insurance policy from $7,500 per year to $10,500 per year. The original premium was already a burden, but he was willing to cut corners on other expenses in order to keep making the payments because that life insurance policy was Jim's intended gift to his children and grandchildren. He viewed it as his final act of generosity for the people he loved more than anything in the world.

With this notice that the premiums would be increasing to an even higher annual amount, he knew the burden would force him into a situation where he would quite literally have to choose whether to purchase his medications next month or pay the premium on his life insurance policy. He called the life insurance company to explore his options.

Jim spoke to a nice person from the company who informed him that he could either keep the policy in force by finding a way to make the higher premium payments on time or he could exercise the option of surrendering his policy. If he chose to surrender the policy, he would receive a cash payment from the company -- known as the policy's "cash surrender value" -- for approximately $10,000.

Ten thousand dollars? Sure, that would be better than zero, but it wouldn't pay Jim's medical bills for long and it certainly wouldn't give him the money he hoped to leave behind for his family when he passed away.

Jim decided to talk it over with his three kids, one of whom is a financial advisor in California. The siblings were unanimous in their feedback: they each had their own families now, they were taking responsibility for their own financial futures, and they didn't want their father to be burdened by the escalating premiums on a life insurance policy. They encouraged him to preserve his money and assured him the life insurance policy, which might have been very important at an earlier time in their dad's life, just wasn't needed anymore.

However, the financial advisor in the family spoke up and told Jim that before he surrendered the policy back to the insurance company for the nominal cash surrender value they were offering, he might want to look into the possibility that his policy might be sold. He told him about something called a "life settlement" that can be a good option for seniors who no longer want or can afford their life insurance policies.

Jim's son went online and found a life settlement broker who is located near his dad in Florida, then checked out the broker's professional credentials and experience to make sure that he seemed qualified to help. The broker talked to Jim the next week and explained the life settlement option to him. Jim agreed to pursue it and directed the broker to explore how much more cash he might receive by selling his policy, rather than accepting the cash surrender value the insurance company offered.

To Jim's great delight, within just a few weeks, the broker obtained three competing bids for his insurance policy. The highest of those bids was for $75,000 . . . more than seven times the amount that Jim would have received if he would have simply surrendered the policy back to the insurance company. Within 90 days, Jim received the check and became the most recent senior to benefit from a life settlement. He paid off some bills and put away enough cash to pay for his medications for years to come. Most of all, he gained some peace of mind.

Economic Pressures on Seniors

Jim's circumstances are not unusual in America. A 2015 report from the National Institute on Retirement Security, "The Continuing Retirement Savings Crisis," confirmed that many Americans are ill-prepared for retirement and are highly anxious about their ability to retire.[1] Many of these folks saw their financial resources eroded substantially by the 2007-2009 financial crisis and have still not been able to recover from that hit.

Just think of some of the noteworthy economic pressures that our seniors are confronting today:

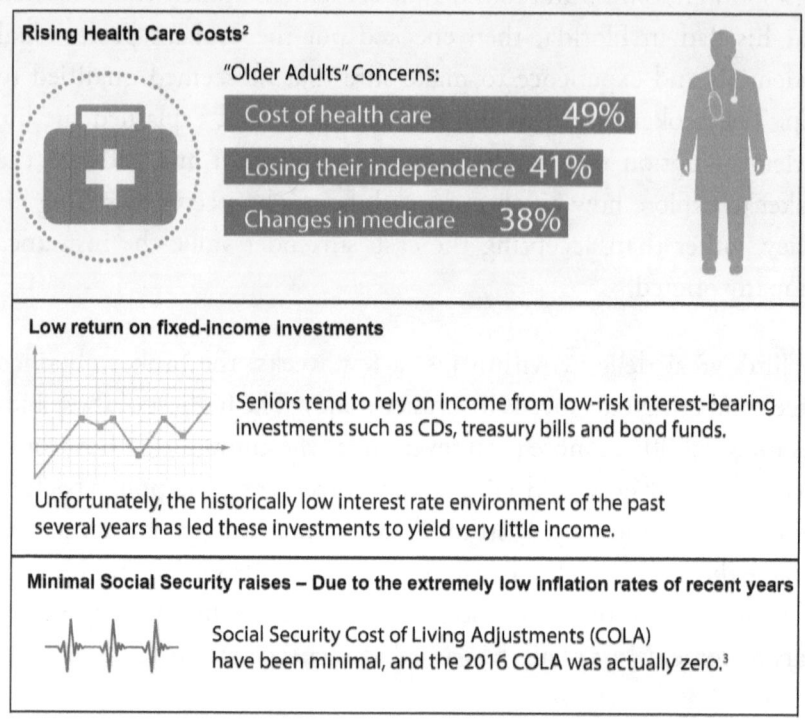

Rising Health Care Costs[2]

"Older Adults" Concerns:

Cost of health care	49%
Losing their independence	41%
Changes in medicare	38%

Low return on fixed-income investments

Seniors tend to rely on income from low-risk interest-bearing investments such as CDs, treasury bills and bond funds.

Unfortunately, the historically low interest rate environment of the past several years has led these investments to yield very little income.

Minimal Social Security raises – Due to the extremely low inflation rates of recent years

Social Security Cost of Living Adjustments (COLA) have been minimal, and the 2016 COLA was actually zero.[3]

With seniors facing such serious financial stresses in retirement, it's no wonder that a recent survey from Wells Fargo found that 22 percent of middle-class Americans say they would rather "die early" than not have enough money to live comfortably in retirement.[4]

Just stop for a moment and let that sink in. We now live in a culture where one in five of our fellow citizens are under such psychological distress due to their retirement savings shortfall that they fear financial ruin more than they fear death.

It's as if our seniors are saying: We haven't saved enough, we don't know what our future needs will be, we can't rely on our investments to produce much income and we don't have enough assets in our names to generate the cash shortfall.

An Overlooked Asset

But what if the secret that Jim learned could be shared with all seniors who are in need of financial relief? What if they knew that a possible untapped asset for providing them with some immediate cash to help defray those retirement expenses may well be right under their noses, lying in a drawer?

The goal of this book is to educate American seniors that their life insurance policies may have economic value to them while they're alive, not just to their beneficiaries when they die. Our purpose is to raise consumer awareness about the choices available for their life insurance policies that may no longer be needed or affordable, especially selling the policy, known as a life settlement.

In the following chapters, we will take you on a brief journey. We'll begin by providing a basic explanation of how a life insurance policy works, then explain the range of options available to policy owners if they no longer need or can afford their policy. We'll proceed by recapping the history of life settlements and describing the various participants in the American life settlements industry, including how seniors are protected by life settlements regulation.

Next, we'll explain who purchases life settlements from seniors and why they do it, and explain who may and who may not be a good candidate for a life settlement. We will help you understand how the value of your policy is determined by potential buyers, then walk through the anatomy of the sale process. The book will close with information about where to go for help in figuring all of this out and determining whether the life settlement option is right for you.

Just to be clear at the outset: the purpose of this book is to educate seniors about options available to them if they have concluded they no longer need or can afford a life insurance policy. It is not our purpose to promote a specific retirement planning strategy and it is certainly not our desire to encourage anyone to sell a life insurance policy they need or want to keep.

Rather, it is our sincere wish that every single American senior be made aware of the alternatives that exist to lapsing or surrendering a life insurance policy back to their insurance company. We thank you for coming along with us on this journey into the emerging marketplace of life settlements.

Chapter One

Your Life Insurance Policy

Have you ever given serious thought to the purpose of your life insurance policy by revisiting the original reason why you purchased a policy in the first place? Do you think of your life insurance policy the same way you analyze other investments in your portfolio of assets? Do you assume the only way that your policy has value to you is when you pass away and the benefits are paid out to your beneficiaries?

These are important questions to ask, given the fact that a life insurance policy is a major financial asset owned by millions of Americans like you, who pay into their policies every single year.

In simple terms, a life insurance policy is a contractual arrangement between the policy owner and the life insurance company that issued the policy. As the policyholder, you determine the amount of life insurance coverage you want (the "death benefit") and then pay the life insurance company a premium to keep the policy in force. The premium may be paid to the life insurance company all at once, with annual payments or perhaps in monthly installments -- but the premium must be paid according to the terms of the policy to keep the life insurance policy active. If you die while the policy is in force, then the life insurance company will pay out the death benefit in one lump sum to the named beneficiary(s) you designated to receive the life insurance benefits.

The Evolution of Life Insurance

Life insurance has been a core part of the American financial landscape since the 1760s, when an insurance company in Charleston, S.C. began offering consumers the opportunity to purchase a basic contract that would pay a cash benefit to the insured's beneficiary upon his or her death. In those early days, life insurance was actually far less popular than flood and fire insurance, and was even a source of controversy in American churches as some religious leaders found it to be an unseemly wager against God.[5]

As the American economy flourished and grew beyond its agrarian roots, life insurance slowly became a more accepted piece of the fabric of financial services offered to consumers. A key element of this growth was a simple message that resonated with many 19th century American men: it's your moral duty to provide for your family. Life insurance began to be viewed as an important vehicle for seeing to it that your family would not be left in poverty in the event of your untimely passing. In other words, it became a bet against death.

In the mid-1800s, the American life insurance industry took off. Indeed, a number of the companies formed during that era are still selling life insurance products today, including New York Life (1845), Mass Mutual (1851), John Hancock (1862) and Met Life (1864).[6] The growth of life insurance sales spiked again following World War I and then again (perhaps ironically) with the onset of the Great Depression. By 1930, there was approximately one policy in place for every adult person in the U.S.

Since that time, as the country's population has ballooned and the demographics have changed significantly, the percentage of Americans who own life insurance has declined. Still, 57 percent of all people in the U.S. were covered by some type of life insurance in 2014, according to LIMRA's 2015 Insurance Barometer Study.[7]

Today, the life insurance industry is a giant part of the American economy. There are 830 U.S. life insurance companies that collectively have 143 million policies in force, with a total "face value" (death benefits) of more than $11.8 trillion. These companies collect more than $110 billion in annual premiums on those life insurance policies.[8]

LIFE INSURANCE FACTS

5 in 10 Americans are covered by some type of life insurance

830 INSURANCE COMPANIES

38 MILLION POLICIES IN-FORCE BY SENIORS

$3+ TRILLION IN DEATH BENEFITS FOR SENIORS

Of course, our focus for this book is on American seniors, and that happens to be a very attractive market for life insurance companies. There are roughly 38 million life insurance policies owned by American seniors, with a total "face value" of more than $3 trillion.[9] Some of these policies were purchased when the insured was a young adult and just starting a family, others were purchased after their kids got older and the financial needs were greater, and others were purchased when the nest was empty.

There are all sorts of life insurance products sold by insurers, but your policy will fall into one of two categories:

1) Term life insurance, which covers you for a specific "term" of years and pays a death benefit only if you die within that term. Term insurance generally offers the largest death benefit for

your premium, however it does not build up cash value and the policy will expire when the term ends.

2) Permanent life insurance, which goes by several names -- such as universal life, variable universal life and whole life. Permanent insurance provides long-term financial protection for you and, in some cases, builds cash savings. However, in order to pay for these benefits, premiums tend to be higher.

Revisiting the Purpose of Life Insurance

Regardless of when you purchased your policy, it's important now to pause for a moment and reflect on the reasons why you purchased that life insurance in the first place. If you're like most seniors, chances are that the appeal of buying a policy was due to one of these considerations:

- To provide an inheritance for your surviving spouse and children;
- To protect your family from debts that would need to be paid;
- To help fund educational expenses for your children or grandchildren;
- To pay for your funeral expenses so your family wouldn't need to front the costs; or
- To leave behind a charitable legacy that your family could carry out on your behalf.

To be sure, there are other legitimate reasons for buying life insurance; some folks might be focused on tax and estate planning, others might have purchased policies as part of business sales or transitions. But did you catch the common thread to each of those items in the list above?

For most of us, the decision to purchase a life insurance policy came down to this basic idea: we were trying to provide financial relief for our loved ones in the event of our untimely death. In fact, a large majority

(84 percent) of Americans believe life insurance is a smart way to care for their family's future.[10]

Life insurance is an important part of the American economy and is a key ingredient in the financial planning process. It's a product that provides us with some peace of mind in knowing that our loved ones will have a financial cushion in the event of our death. For many of our families, life insurance has been one of the core assets we hold for years.

INSURANCE POLICY FACTS

88%

of Universal life insurance polices never actually result in a death claim

But did you know that nearly 88 percent of universal life insurance policies and almost 85 percent of term life insurance policies never actually result in a death claim?[11]

Today, many seniors are in a different place than when they first purchased their life insurance policies. Our kids turn into adults and begin their own families, assuming the personal financial responsibilities that each generation of parents has to provide for their own kids. At the same time, our income tapers off in retirement as we become increasingly reliant on Social Security and whatever savings we have left.

For many of us, the reason we bought that life insurance policy in the first place -- to provide financial relief for our families -- may no longer apply like it once did. And for others of us, those annual premiums that were once just another expense in the family budget, may now be posing a financial burden.

The message should be that your life insurance policy is a very important investment, just as your other financial assets. As such, it should be reviewed and evaluated as to its purpose and place in your financial plan.

Chapter Two

What if You Don't Need or Can't Afford Your Policy?

Since the introduction of life insurance products to the U.S., Americans have primarily purchased life insurance policies to provide financial relief to our loved ones in the event of our deaths. To that end, by the very nature of a life insurance policy, a consumer will always obtain the maximum financial benefit from a policy by keeping it in-force until they pass away. At that time, the beneficiaries of the policy will receive the full death benefit from the life insurance company.

Let's restate this simple principle more bluntly: you will always obtain the greatest benefit from your life insurance policy for your heirs by keeping the policy until you die. This fact is undisputed.

However, as we saw in the story discussed in the Introduction to this book, we can't always anticipate what life is going to throw our way. The truth is that many seniors find themselves confronting unexpected life changes that have a major impact on their financial circumstances, including the way they think about their life insurance policies.

Can't Afford It or Don't Need It Anymore?

There are a number of reasons why you might be driven to reassess whether it makes sense for you to keep your life insurance policy. Perhaps the most common one is if you simply can't afford the premiums on the policy any longer. This may be the result of rising living expenses or it might be due to declining retirement income. Unfortunately, there is a third factor that can make life insurance premiums unaffordable for seniors: some life insurance companies occasionally increase the premiums themselves.

Business publications such as the Wall Street Journal[12] and Insurance News Net[13] have reported that certain life insurers -- stung by lower than expected returns on their own corporate investments -- have shocked consumers by sending them letters that notified them of increases in their premiums. These increases have been significant, some as high as 200 percent. What is especially troubling is that at least one carrier acknowledged the premium hikes were targeted at consumers over the age of 70.[14]

To be fair, state regulators and government officials typically do their best to protect consumers from unfair business practices; but there is always a risk that one day you may receive a letter delivering a similar shock, rendering your premiums no longer affordable.

Another factor that causes seniors to reassess whether they still need their life insurance policies is if you no longer need the death benefit for your heirs. For many individuals, particularly those who may be the primary income providers for their families, at least for a season of life, life insurance provided an important peace of mind that our spouses and kids would have a financial cushion in the event of our sudden passing. But as life marches on and our kids leave the nest, starting families of their own, they take personal responsibility for the financial needs of their spouses and kids. Many seniors choose to keep their life insurance policies in force as a form of estate planning for their grandkids, but other seniors conclude that the financial cushion they sought to provide for their kids when they were young is just no longer necessary.

There are other factors that cause seniors to evaluate the cost of maintaining their life insurance policies in the context of competing expenses. This cuts two ways. On the one hand, the money left in your budget to pay those annual life insurance premiums may be under greater stress due to other essential expenses that are rising. At the same time, you may be evaluating all of your available assets as potential vehicles for generating cash -- and remember, from our discussion in Chapter One, that a life insurance policy is one of your assets.

For example, many seniors are grappling with rising health care bills. This problem is especially acute in situations where an elderly person has prescription medication needs that are not fully covered by Medicare's prescription drug benefit (or other private insurance plan), creating a monthly financial obligation that was never anticipated. Another example might be long-term care expenses for one or both of the spouses in a marriage. These costs can be steep and the specific insurance policies that fund long-term care are typically very expensive.

Of course, some factors that play a role in the decision to reassess life insurance policies are less dire and all about quality of life! For instance, you might simply be looking to reduce your financial outlays and increase your available cash to fund your retirement lifestyle expenses. Some seniors discover that retirement suits them quite nicely and they become more cognizant of how fleeting the "golden years" can be, prompting them to take trips and seek out experiences that all come with price tags. You may be dreaming about the additional adventures you could plan in retirement if you were able to eliminate the expense of keeping your life insurance policy in force and instead use it to generate cash for your retirement fund.

And there are other factors that are just related to financial planning considerations. For example, maybe you own a term life insurance policy that is nearing the end of its coverage period and you're trying to determine whether it's worthwhile to convert it for another term. Or maybe you recently sold a business and the life insurance policy you had in place is no longer required to protect your investors, lenders or employees.

You Have Options!

Regardless of the reason(s) that may apply to your situation, if you decide that you no longer need or can no longer afford your life insurance policy, there is good news that you need to hear: you have options to consider for what to do with that policy.

For decades, most seniors in this situation have simply defaulted to a "lapse" or "surrender" of the policy back to the insurance company.[15] A life insurance policy will lapse when premiums are not paid on the policy and there isn't any cash contained in the policy. In this scenario, there is literally a "lapse in coverage" and the policy will no longer pay out a death benefit if the insured person dies. A policy is surrendered when the owner cancels the policy and requests for the insurance company to pay them the "cash surrender value" sitting in the policy, minus any administrative fees.

The number and amount of lapsed life insurance policies by Americans over the age of 65 is staggering: more than 250,000 policies with a combined face value of more than $57 billion are lapsed and surrendered back to life carriers each year. The average face value of those policies is approximately $225,000.[16] And that only includes universal and variable life policies; if term life and whole life policies are added, the total exceeds $112 billion.

	UL & VL LAPSE/SURRENDER ONLY FOR AGES 65+ ONLY Estimates based on 2008 Data | Source: LIMRA/SOA 2012 Persistency Study					
Age Group	**Total Inforce**			**Annual Lapses**		
	# of Policies	Face Value	AVG FV	# of Policies	Face Value	AVG FV
65-69	2,358,650	$ 500,389,150,000	$212,151	110,675	$24,337,733,500	$ 219,903
70-74	1,516,625	$ 350,363,075,000	$231,015	65,090	$14,143,920,863	$ 217,297
75-79	1,024,604	$ 289,771,262,500	$282,813	43,063	$10,788,689,206	$ 250,535
80-84	605,634	$ 188,709,350,000	$311,590	24,059	$ 6,036,365,750	$ 250,894
85-89	271,873	$ 74,939,693,750	$275,643	9,484	$ 1,605,402,944	$ 169,271
90-94	28,403	$ 12,521,062,500	$440,832	994	$ 208,684,375	$ 209,920
95-100	-	$ -	$ -	-	$ -	$ -
Age 65+	5,805,789	$1,416,693,593,750	$244,014	253,365	$57,120,796,638	$ 225,448

Data and analysis courtesy of Welcome Funds (http://www.welcomefunds.com)

So, if a senior has decided they no longer need or can afford a life insurance policy, what are the alternatives to just lapsing the policy and surrendering it back to the insurance company?

Here are some options that you need to know exist:

- Maintain the policy by obtaining loans to cover your premiums, using the policy or its cash surrender value as collateral;

- Seek what is called an "accelerated death benefit" (ADB), whereby some carriers may allow you to obtain a portion of your death benefit while you're still alive;

- Assign the policy to someone else as a gift or to a non-profit organization as a charitable contribution;

- If it is a "term" policy, attempt to convert it to permanent insurance;

- Reduce the death benefit on the policy in exchange for a reduction in your annual premiums; and

- Sell the policy to a third-party investor through what is known as a life settlement.

As with any financial planning decision, there is no "one size fits all" answer to which of these options is best. The one that makes the most sense for you will depend on your unique needs and desires.

But according to the research, if the motivating consideration for you is to obtain cash in your hands -- for retirement needs, health care expenses or simply to invest into other assets -- then a life settlement is likely the best alternative. Why?

It's very simple: when seniors enter into a life settlement, they realize an average of seven times the amount of the policy's cash surrender value, based on an analysis of a survey by the U.S. Government Accountability Office.[17] That means for every $1,000 you will receive by surrendering your policy back to the insurance company, on average, you will receive $7,000 by selling your life insurance policy to an investor.

If this is the case, then why do most seniors default to the option of simply lapsing or surrendering their life insurance policies back to the companies that sold the policies to them? Quite frankly, it's because they are not aware of the possibility that it may be sold!

Seniors Have the Right to Know

A survey by the Insurance Studies Institute reported that less than 50 percent of seniors are aware of the option to consider selling their life policy.[18] Further, 90 percent of seniors who had lapsed a policy would have considered selling it if they had known a life settlement was an option.

Sadly, a large number of the professionals often responsible for informing seniors about these sorts of crucial financial options -- their trusted financial advisors -- are themselves unaware that a policy may be sold as a life settlement. One study found that 49 percent of financial advisors lack knowledge about life settlements and, therefore, do not recommend the option. In addition, 23 percent said they are actually prohibited from engaging in a life settlement transaction by their insurance company.[19]

Did you catch that? Nearly one in four professional financial advisors aren't even allowed to tell you about the fact that you have the right to sell your life insurance policy because the life insurance industry doesn't want that option to be known to you. These are the same people whom you trusted enough to purchase your policy from them in the first place.

It's time for this lack of awareness to be corrected once and for all. It's time for all American seniors who own life insurance to be fully informed of all their options. We now have the research to document how common it is for seniors to lapse or surrender their life insurance policies back to the insurance companies and we have new data demonstrating that life settlements deliver substantially more cash to consumers. That means we have a benchmark for the serious amount of financial value available to seniors from the possible sale of their policies.

The time has come for the American financial services industry to educate seniors about the alternatives available to lapsing a life insurance policy they no longer need or can no longer afford.

Chapter Three

The Life Settlement Option

After considering all of the options available to you, if you decide to sell a life insurance policy you no longer need or can afford, you may do so through what is known as a life settlement.

A life settlement is the sale of an existing life insurance policy to a third party for more than its cash surrender value but less than its death benefit. In a life settlement transaction, the policy's owner transfers the policy to the buyer in exchange for an immediate cash payment. At this point, the buyer becomes the named owner of record with the insurance company that issued the life insurance policy, pays all future premium payments and then receives the benefit upon the death of the insured person.

The Legal Foundation

So, what makes it possible for you to sell your life insurance policy as a life settlement? The legal basis that allows the sale of a policy as a legitimate option for life insurance owners may be found in a century-old U.S. Supreme Court opinion, *Grigsby v. Russell,* which was decided in 1911.[20]

The case centered on Dr. A.H. Grigsby, who treated a patient named John C. Burchard. As a way to raise the cash he needed to pay his medical bill, Mr. Burchard offered to sell Dr. Grigsby his life insurance policy for $100; Dr. Grigsby would then pay the remaining premiums on the policy and collect the benefit upon Mr. Burchard's death. Dr. Grigsby agreed and the transaction was completed. When Mr. Burchard passed away a year later, Dr. Grigsby tried to collect the benefit – but an executor of Burchard's estate (R.L. Russell) challenged him in court and won. The case eventually reached the U.S. Supreme Court, where Justice Oliver Wendell Holmes Jr. delivered the opinion of the court.

The crux of Justice Holmes' opinion was this: "So far as reasonable safety permits, it is desirable to give to life policies the ordinary characteristics of property. To deny the right to sell except to persons having such an interest is to diminish appreciably the value of the contract in the owner's hands."[21]

Justice Holmes' decision established the fundamental principle upon which the life settlement industry would eventually be based: a life insurance policy is private property that can be assigned (sold) at the will of the owner. This legal precedent has been reinforced in the decades since the *Grigsby* decision, most recently in the passage of the Health Insurance Portability and Accountability Act (HIPAA) in 1996. Signed into law by President Clinton, HIPAA allowed the owner and/ or beneficiary of a life insurance policy to transfer the ownership and/ or beneficial interest in that policy to a third party.[22]

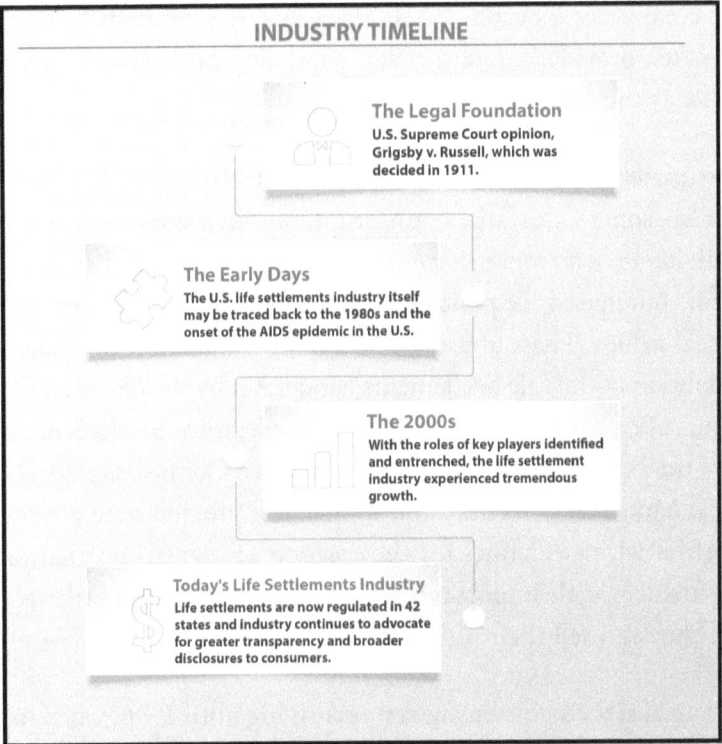

INDUSTRY TIMELINE

The Legal Foundation
U.S. Supreme Court opinion, Grigsby v. Russell, which was decided in 1911.

The Early Days
The U.S. life settlements industry itself may be traced back to the 1980s and the onset of the AIDS epidemic in the U.S.

The 2000s
With the roles of key players identified and entrenched, the life settlement industry experienced tremendous growth.

Today's Life Settlements Industry
Life settlements are now regulated in 42 states and industry continues to advocate for greater transparency and broader disclosures to consumers.

The Early Days

The U.S. life settlements industry itself may be traced back to the 1980s and the onset of the AIDS epidemic in the U.S. At that time, most people who contracted the HIV virus eventually suffered from AIDS; those patients faced an extremely short life expectancy. Often, these individuals owned life insurance policies. It was under these circumstances that the first "viatical" settlements were created.

Viatical settlements are similar but not the same as life settlements. For a viatical settlement, a person who is selling his/her policy is terminally or chronically ill and expected to live less than two years. A viatical settlement offered someone with a terminal illness an opportunity to generate immediate cash from a life insurance policy in order to provide some measure of financial cushion to pay for end-of-life medical expenses. For many AIDS patients, the proceeds from viatical settlements provided much-needed psychological comfort that was as valuable as the financial payment.

Unfortunately, during the beginning era of viatical settlements, there were also some cases where unscrupulous investors took advantage of individuals who were in poor health and financial distress. Those investors purchased the policies of some individuals for prices far below their real values. These abuses provided the foundation that later led to the adoption of the Life Settlements Model Act by the National Council of Insurance Legislators (NCOIL) and the Viatical Settlements Model Act by the National Association of Insurance Commissioners (NAIC) Viatical Model Act.[23] These two model acts provide state government authorities with guidelines for the creation of regulations that provide policy owners with important protections and a safer marketplace in which they can sell their policies.

The viatical settlements business was thriving until 1996, when medical researchers announced the development of a "cocktail" combination of pharmaceutical drugs that extended the lives of AIDS patients for an unknown number of years. This important medical breakthrough changed the life expectancy assumptions upon which viatical settlements had been based.

So, as medical advancements made it possible to prolong the lives of those who contracted HIV -- and individuals dealing with other life-threatening illnesses -- viatical settlements became less common, mostly because investors would no longer buy policies that would likely need to be held for longer periods of time.

The 2000s

In 2000, NCOIL adopted the "Life Settlements Model Act" and, over the course of the next few years, the purchase of life insurance policies from senior citizens became widely known as "life settlements" transactions.

The NAIC Model Act was also amended extensively. New sections were added to address fraud, advertising and civil remedies.

By 2005, life settlements had quickly grown to a multibillion-dollar industry (measured by total value of policies settled) as seniors discovered they could obtain significantly more value from selling their policies than from surrendering them to the insurance companies.

During 2005-2006, a new life insurance concept gained some traction known as Stranger-Originated Life Insurance (STOLI). STOLI was based on the idea that a person could have a life insurance policy issued on his or her own life, borrow the funds to pay for the premiums and then sell the policy two years later to an investor. The strategy was to sell the policy for enough money to pay off the loan and pocket a profit.

Unfortunately, what happened was a number of investors concocted plans to enlist life insurance agents who would recruit clients and work with them to apply for very large life insurance policies ($5-$10+ million). The policies were pre-planned to be sold as life settlements after the two-year "non-contestability" period ended.

STOLI transactions were deemed illegal and aggressive efforts were undertaken to pass legislation to end the practice; indeed, today most states have regulations that ban STOLI.

In the late-2000s, the financial crisis took its toll on the industry, but in the process it brought into focus the need for seniors to find new sources of cash to fund their retirements. A 2009 study conducted by Golden Gateway Financial, Inc. and the Insurances Studies Institute illustrated the opportunity for growth, finding that "80% of seniors owned some form of life insurance policy, but nearly half are unaware it can be sold for cash now."[24]

Today's Life Settlements Industry

Out of this era, the life settlements industry emerged from an important realization that the concept of selling a life insurance policy could make sense for older people. As a result, life settlements became the accepted term for the process of seniors selling their life insurance policies on the "secondary market" to investors who would pay cash for that policy.

There are four key participants in the life settlements industry, each of whom plays an important role:

1) **Consumers**

   The first and most important player is you, the consumer who owns a life insurance policy you've decided that you no longer need or can afford. You hold the keys to the asset that makes the entire industry happen, which means you are entitled to certain regulatory protections and you have the power to determine whether or not to put your policy up for sale.

2) **Brokers**

   Life settlement brokers are professionals who "shop" a consumer's life insurance policy to a number of providers, much like how a real estate broker shows your home to a number of potential buyers. It's not essential to go through a broker in order to sell a life insurance policy, but consumers who do so will find that the brokers collect bids and help their clients evaluate the offers based on various criteria (e.g., the purchase price and how long the transaction will take) and then receive their fees once the transaction is completed. However, compensation arrangements can vary significantly, so they should be fully disclosed and understood in advance. In states that regulate life settlements, there are laws pertaining to broker responsibilities that may subject the broker to penalties if violated.[25]

3) Providers

Life settlement providers serve as the "buyers" in a life settlement transaction and these are the players who are responsible for paying you an amount of cash that is greater than your policy's cash surrender value. The top providers in the industry are experienced in the analysis of life insurance policies and carefully review the transaction details on behalf of the institutional investors who provide the funding to purchase policies from consumers.[26] In 42 states and the territory of Puerto Rico, life settlement providers must be licensed where the policy owner resides and must follow specific rules.

4) Investors

Life settlement investors are the companies that provide the funding in a life settlement transaction so a life insurance policy can be purchased. Some life settlement investors use their own capital to purchase the policies, others may raise the capital from a pool of investors. We'll go into more detail on this subject later in the book, but what you need to know is that the major life settlement investors are large institutional investment firms that have deep pockets and substantial assets behind them. These are professional investors who know what they're doing and understand that life settlements are legitimate transactions that represent good value for everyone involved.

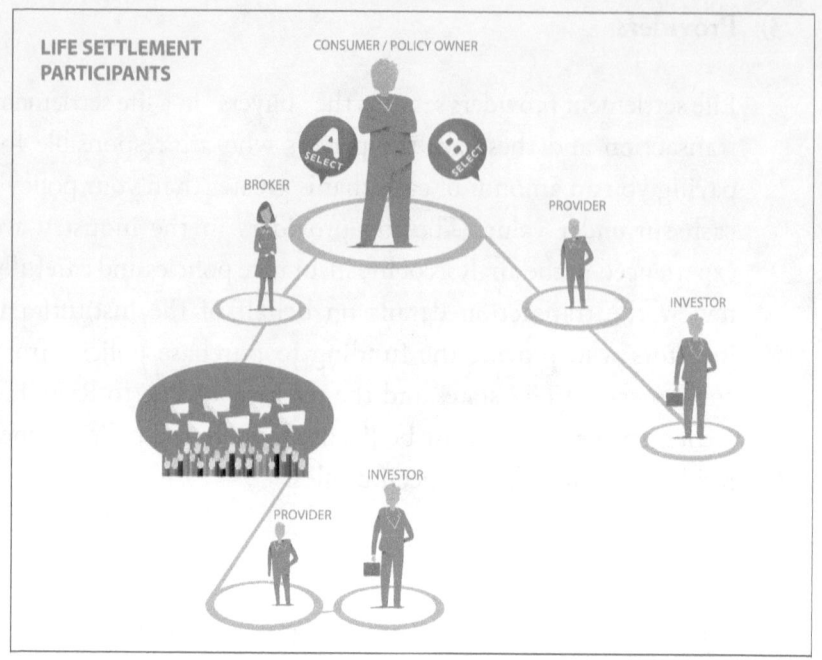

The Growth

With the roles of these four key players identified and entrenched, the life settlement industry experienced tremendous growth throughout the 2000s. However, when the economic crisis hit in 2008-2009, the industry was dealt a tremendous setback as capital suddenly dried up and there was little funding available for purchasing policies. As with many other sectors of the American economy, it took a few years for the dramatic impact of this Great Recession to slowly dissipate in the life settlement industry.

But in 2011, as capital markets renewed their interest in life settlements, the market began its resurgence. In the years that followed, life settlement transactions picked up and major investors -- such as Berkshire Hathaway, various pension funds and a few large hedge funds -- returned to the industry.[27] By 2014, life settlement transaction volumes were reported higher by market participants in all major segments of the industry and independent analysts from Conning & Co. forecast "growing unmet need and increasing opportunity" for life settlement transactions in the years to come.[28]

A key driver of this growth has been the evolution of the industry from its early days as essentially an innovative financial planning option to what it is today: a maturing business with strong regulatory oversight.

Life settlements are now regulated in 42 states, providing 90 percent of the U.S. population with protection under comprehensive laws that establish important boundaries for how life insurance policies may be sold by consumers.[29] For example, these laws require conditions such as the following:

- Waiting periods before you can sell a life insurance policy
- Transparency on costs involved in the transaction
- Licensing requirements for life settlement brokers and providers
- Consumer privacy safeguards

Specifically, most states require policy owners to receive disclosure of the compensation paid to brokers. In addition, most states require that consumers receive all offers and counteroffers, alternatives to settlements, and risks related to taxation and government assistance that may relate to the sale of their policies. Many states also require life settlement companies to follow rigorous anti-fraud plans that ensure the policies they purchase are legitimate. The result of these formal regulations is that all of the players in the industry (consumers, providers, brokers and investors) are able to be confident that they're participating in an orderly marketplace.

In fact, according to the NAIC Consumer Information Source, since the start of 2012, only two consumer complaints involving settlements have been reported nationally.[30] This is an amazing indication that consumers are being well-protected by the industry's ethical guidelines and the states' regulatory requirements, enabling seniors to feel confident about life settlements as an attractive option for what to do with a life insurance policy they no longer need or can afford.

Still, the life settlement industry continues to advocate for greater transparency and broader disclosures to consumers. For example, there is a growing chorus of voices calling for life insurance companies to be required to inform a policy owner about the life settlement option before they lapse a policy. This "Seniors' Right to Know" movement is gaining momentum in several states.[31] Another advocacy effort involves "Medicaid Life Settlements Act" legislation, which would give citizens applying for Medicaid the right to sell their life insurance policies for more money than the cash surrender value from the insurance company, and apply that cash toward long-term care services, home health care, assisted living and nursing home services or support.[32]

These and other efforts are likely to accelerate greater opportunities for seniors to sell their life insurance policies in a safe and regulated marketplace.

Chapter Four

Who Buys the Policies?

Have you ever spent a fun weekend afternoon at a "flea market" where you shopped around and kept your eyes open for a hidden bargain? Or maybe cruised through your neighborhood on a Saturday morning, checking out garage sales for antiques to add to your living room?

These are classic American examples of free markets, where you have sellers of goods who are seeking to find interested buyers of those goods. The key factor that brings sellers and buyers together is price: is the buyer willing to pay the seller a high enough price in order for both parties to feel they are receiving the value they need to complete a transaction?

For any market to work, there must be satisfied buyers and satisfied sellers. If the value scale tips too far toward one or the other, the market will not thrive and will eventually decline. We see this play out every day in our own communities, as restaurants whose prices were too high for consumers to afford eventually go out of business or video rental stores close down because we found greater value downloading movies from the comfort of our own homes.

This same dynamic is true in the life settlements market. In order for seniors to be able to obtain attractive cash payments for their unwanted or unaffordable life insurance policies, there has to be a buyer on the other end of those transactions. In turn, that buyer must be able to achieve good value from the investment they're making in the purchase of the policies or they won't have any incentive to continue buying more policies.

Institutional Investors in Life Settlements

A study from Conning, Inc. found that investors purchased $1.7 billion worth of U.S. life insurance ("face value") during 2014, bringing the total active life settlements market to more than $32 billion at the start of 2015.[33] The analysts projected that "continued steady growth" in life settlements will continue for the coming years.

Just who is buying all of these policies? In short, the vast majority of life settlement transactions are funded by institutional investors -- that is, sophisticated financing entities tasked with managing large pools of capital for various investors in a way that will maximize their investment returns. There have always been a number of highly regarded institutional investors in the life settlements market, but in recent years there has been a steady influx of more funds into the space. Some of these leading institutional investors who serve as buyers in the life settlements market include major pension funds, endowments, foundations and investment banks.

This illustrates that life settlements are not only attractive options for seniors who no longer need or can afford their life insurance policies, but also for investors who are seeking attractive returns by purchasing those policies. In other words, life settlements are producing satisfied sellers and satisfied buyers, a key to a healthy market.

Life settlement investors may use their own capital to purchase life insurance policies or they may raise the capital from various investors. As we saw in Chapter Three, the life settlement provider is the one who actually enters into the transaction with the consumer and makes the cash payment for the policy when the life settlement transaction closes. In most cases, the life settlement provider has an agreement with an institutional investor to provide the funds needed to acquire the policy; in some cases, the life settlement provider is also the investor and uses its own capital to purchase the policy.

An Attractive Asset Class

When properly structured and consummated, life settlements can be true "win-win" financial transactions: seniors obtain a cash payment for an insurance policy that is much greater than what the insurance company would give them if they lapsed or surrendered the policy, while investors obtain attractive returns that allow them to make good money on the purchase of those policies with little risk that their principal will be lost.

There are three major reasons why institutional investors have invested billions of dollars into life settlements[34]:

- Excellent Returns

Life settlements have captured the interest of professional investors because they consistently offer double-digit returns on their investments. According to an 11-year study by The London School of Business, investors purchasing their sample of life settlements could have expected to earn an average internal rate of return of 12.5 percent per year.[35] The lowest year produced an 11.0 percent return, the highest year produced an 18.9 percent return. That is a very attractive gain for an investor.

- Principal is Safe

When institutions invest in life settlements, they don't need to worry about losing their principal, as they often do with other assets they purchase. Although they can never predict with certainty how many years will go by before any one individual life insurance policy in their portfolio "matures" and the death benefit is collected, they do know with certainty that day will eventually come. So there is minimal risk of their principal investment being lost.

- Stability of Investment

The reason that institutional investors are especially drawn to life settlements now is that they have learned those returns are not tied to the performance of other economic engines, such as the stock market, the housing sector, the political climate or what the Federal Reserve is doing with interest rates. A life settlement is called a "non-correlated asset" -- meaning the returns aren't correlated or tied to other factors beyond the investor's control -- and those kinds of investments are in great demand for professional money managers because they allow them to reduce the volatility in their overall portfolios.[36]

What Risks Do Investors Take?

You might ask what risks there are for investors when they buy your insurance policy, especially in light of the returns that may appear to be greater than for some other investment classes. When someone buys your insurance policy, assumes all future premium payments and receives the death benefit when the policy matures, there are indeed certain risks they must consider.

First of all, a life settlement is basically an "illiquid" investment. This means that it can't easily be sold for cash without a substantial loss in value. When an investor purchases your policy, they don't receive annual interest payments or dividends, as with bond and stock investments. In fact, each year they must make additional investments to pay the premium payments to keep the policy active. The payoff that creates the attractive return doesn't come until the policy matures and the death benefit is paid, making it illiquid compared with alternative investments.

A second risk factor for the investor is the possibility of the person insured under the policy to live longer than estimated, sometimes significantly longer. As a result, the investor may have to make additional annual premium payments and wait perhaps years to receive the death benefit, thus reducing the return on the investment. (On the other hand, in some cases, the insured may pass away sooner than expected, increasing the return.)

Finally, there is some risk that life insurance companies may unexpectedly increase annual payments, causing the investor to pay significantly more in premiums than planned when the policy was purchased. This risk factor has played out in recent years, with some insurers raising premiums on elderly policy owners with very little advance notice.[37]

While these are risks that an institutional investor must assume when they make investments in portfolios of life settlements, the characteristics of a life settlement investment offset other risks from other asset classes, thus making them attractive.

Beware of Investing in Life Settlements Yourself!

We would be remiss if we didn't pause for a moment to address a common misunderstanding – especially with articles and blog posts you may find on the Internet – in the world of life settlements. The confusion often arises when people misunderstand the difference between a life settlement transaction (selling a life insurance policy that may no longer be needed or affordable) and a life settlement investment (buying a life insurance policy, or a "fractional" interest in a policy, for an investment return).[38]

As attractive as life settlements are for institutional investors, they're just not appropriate investments for consumers. Unfortunately, there are some companies out there that have successfully persuaded many individuals to pull money out of their retirement accounts or personal savings in order to invest in life settlements through "fractionalized shares" in pools of life insurance policies that have been purchased. Sadly, many individual investors have been scammed by these unethical business ventures and lost some or all of their money.

Life settlements are complicated assets for investment purposes because they require highly skilled professionals to analyze the value of each policy and determine a price that is fair to both the buyer and the seller. Moreover, the buyer must have extremely deep pockets that allows them to own a huge number of policies at one time so they can spread out the risk from any one individual policy being held for a longer amount of time than was expected. Finally, the buyer must have the patience and discipline required to bring a long-term perspective to their investment goals, avoiding a predicament where they need to exit their investment quickly in order to pay their own bills. Funds must often be committed for several years, unlike a mutual fund that people can buy and sell on virtually any day of their choosing.

For all of these reasons, life settlements are simply not appropriate for individual investors. In fact, the Life Insurance Settlement Association (LISA) has even adopted a position that this marketplace is not appropriate for individual investors acting on their own. LISA affirms that the primary buyers of life settlements should be institutional investors -- such as pension funds, endowments, foundations and private equity funds -- and specifically advises against any individuals investing their retirement savings in life settlements.[39]

Again, keep in mind that any news stories you hear or articles you read about individuals investing in life settlements has absolutely no connection whatsoever to life settlement transactions, the sale of policies by the policy owners. Those are two entirely unrelated issues and they shouldn't be conflated.

The bottom line is that for the right kind of investor, backed by significant capital and professional managers, life settlements are a very attractive asset class that can produce excellent returns on their money. This creates the necessary incentive for ensuring a steady flow of interested buyers of seniors' unwanted or unaffordable life insurance policies, a key ingredient for a healthy market with satisfied sellers and buyers alike.

Chapter Five

Candidates for Life Settlements

We've established that life settlements are an attractive option for seniors who no longer need or can afford their life insurance policies, and we've explained how the life settlement industry has evolved into a safe and regulated marketplace for both buyers and sellers of policies. At this point, you may be thinking to yourself, "All of my friends need to get in on this opportunity and sell their policies for cash in their hands now!"

Well, not so fast.

Not for Everyone

Life settlements are not for everyone. First of all, as we explained in Chapter Two, there is a basic principle about life insurance that all seniors should understand: you will always obtain the greatest benefit from your life insurance policy for your heirs by keeping the policy until you die. So if you want your beneficiary to obtain the full death benefit from your life insurance policy, then by all means you should keep it!

Even for those who would like to explore selling their life insurance policies, there are a few things that will pretty much eliminate the feasibility of a life settlement for some folks. The most common disqualifying factor is age. If you are younger than 65, it's unlikely your policy will find value in the secondary market that will be greater than the cash surrender value from the insurance company. In fact, even if you are in your late-60s and in good health, it may be tough to find someone willing to pay enough for your policy to make it worthwhile to sell.[40] The possible exception to the minimum age requirement is if you have serious medical problems that significantly shorten your life expectancy.

The next most frequent criterion that can take a life settlement off the table is the size of your life insurance policy. If the death benefit on the policy is less than $100,000, it may not attract a lot of interest from potential buyers -- and realistically, policies that have a face value of at least $200,000 generate the most meaningful offers. This may change in the years to come, but at this point the life settlement providers who are buying life insurance policies have essentially set the minimum bar at that six-figure mark.

Another factor that may reduce the appeal of life settlements for some seniors is the tax implications from the sale of a life insurance policy. A 2009 IRS ruling established some complex regulations governing the amount of income recognized by a taxpayer upon the surrender or sale of a life insurance contract.[41] According to most legal interpretations of this ruling, some of the proceeds of a life settlement are almost certainly taxable. If this tax burden reduces the proceeds from the sale too much, then a life settlement may not be feasible.

Moreover, the proceeds of a life settlement could also be subject to the claims of creditors in the event of a bankruptcy petition. This is an important consideration for any senior contemplating a restructuring of their debt and assets since laws on the books now require bankruptcy trustees to maximize the value of life insurance policies for the benefit of creditors.[42]

The Best Candidates

There are obviously a number of seniors for whom a life settlement is not a feasible option, but what are the factors that make someone a good candidate for a life settlement transaction?

To be blunt, life expectancy is the key component in determining the market value of a life settlement transaction; the shorter the life expectancy, the more attractive the policy is to a buyer. This is because the longer a person is projected to live, the greater the amount of premiums that need to be paid and the longer the investor must wait to collect the death benefit. So the senior's current age, projected life expectancy and health condition are all critical factors in determining if the policy owner is a good candidate for a life settlement.

There are also some financial considerations regarding the type of insurance policy under review that will determine whether the senior is a good candidate for a settlement. All types of life insurance policies could qualify for sale in the life settlement market, but universal life policies and term life policies are the most commonly purchased policies because they tend to enable the buyers to make the most compelling offers to seniors.

Universal life policies are ideal for life settlements, even if the policy has become "underfunded" and the owner is facing a premium increase in order to keep the policy in force[43]. This is because many universal life policies allow buyers to pay minimum premiums based on the value of the policy, which means investors can reduce their cash outlays and maximize their returns. Term life policies can also be excellent candidates for settlements if they are nearing the end of their terms and are able to be converted to a whole or universal life policy by the buyer of the policy. This allows the senior to avoid the higher premiums they'd have to pay by taking on a new policy -- instead receiving a cash payment for selling it to someone else -- and allows the investor to take ownership of an asset with a large payout down the road.

To sum up, the best candidates for life settlements are life insurance policy owners who meet the following criteria:

BEST CANDIDATES FOR A LIFE SETTLEMENT

1. Age 65 or older

2. One or more health issues

3. Life expectancy of less than 12 years

4. Policy with a death benefit of $100,000 or more

5. Universal Life or Convertible Term Life policy

It's important to stress that a life settlement may still be an option for lots of seniors who fail to meet one or more of these ideal criteria. For example, there are creative ways to sell part of the death benefit in your policy and still retain part of it for your heirs. There are some life settlement providers who are willing to look at your policy even if the face value is as low as $50,000. And there are a number of investors out there who have been known to make offers on policies with all sorts of structures, including "joint survivorship" policies and group life policies. There is no single uniform formula for which policies can be sold and which can not. Still, the truth is that some seniors are better candidates for life settlements than others.

Life settlements may not be for everyone who no longer need or can afford their life insurance policies, but for the senior who meets the criteria of being a good candidate, a life settlement is a substantially better option than lapsing or surrendering a policy back to the insurance company.

Chapter Six

How Much is Your Policy Worth?

Back in Chapter One, we explained that your life insurance policy is legally recognized as your personal property. That means it's an asset you own and can hold for its originally intended purpose of paying out a death benefit to your heirs one day.

But if you no longer want or can afford that policy and have made a decision to sell it through a life settlement, the first thing you're going to want to know is how much it's worth! It may be helpful to understand the potential value of your policy by starting with a mindset that selling a life insurance policy is similar to selling any other personal asset. The marketplace determines how much it is worth.

Factors that Influence Value

Any asset that you own has certain characteristics that influence its value. For example, the value of your home is determined by things such as location, style, size and demand for homes in your area. The value of one share of a company's stock is determined by investors' perceptions about the economy and growth prospects of the company, the amount of dividends it pays to investors, and estimates of how much the price will increase over time. The value of a bond investment is determined by the quality of the company issuing the debt, how much annual interest it pays and when the bond matures or when the investor will receive the final payment.

Likewise, the value of a life insurance policy has characteristics that determine its value; these are factors that are unique to life settlements and different from other investments.[44] Basically, three factors determine how much a life insurance policy is worth:

1) The Policy Size

What is the "death benefit" of your policy? That is the starting point because it's the amount of money the potential buyers of the policy can expect to collect on their investment when the death benefit is paid.

2) The Maintenance Costs

What are the annual premiums on your policy? That tells the potential buyers how much it will cost them each year to keep the policy in force.

3) Your Age and Health

How old are you and do you have any health issues? These factors are important because they determine your "life expectancy" -- which in turn allows potential buyers of your policy to project how long they'll be paying those premiums before collecting on the benefit.

There is a simple rule of thumb that always determines the market value of a life insurance policy: the higher the death benefit, the lower the premiums and the shorter the life expectancy the greater the value of the policy in a life settlement. That's it, there's nothing mysterious involved.

Calculating a Price

There is no official price menu to which you can refer in determining precisely how much your policy is worth right now on the "secondary market" for life insurance. The reason for this is that the final piece of the puzzle in calculating a price for your policy, just like a lot of other personal property items you own, is determining how much a buyer is willing to spend in order to get the value they're seeking in their investment.

In a nutshell, investors must decide how much they can afford to pay for your life insurance policy today to earn the rate of return they want to receive, considering that they have to pay the annual premiums for the remainder of your lifetime.[45] The investment term used to determine the calculation of this appropriate price is "discounting" and it works something like this:

Let's say an investor has the opportunity to make an investment into something that will pay out $100,000 at the end of seven years. The investor decides that he wants to earn a 10% annual return on that investment over the course of those seven years. Based on the math of internal rates of return, the investor would need to pay no more than $51,316 today in order to earn an annual return of at least 10% for those seven years.

The concept of "discounting" for valuing a life insurance policy is similar, except for one additional variable. In order to keep the policy active, annual premiums will need to be paid to the insurance company, representing additional investments. So, if we assume that premiums of $2,500 must be paid by the investor every year to keep the policy active -- and the same 10% return is desired on the premium investments -- then the investor needs to tack-on another $26,090 in projected costs over those seven years. That means the costs to an investor to purchase this asset come to $77,406.

So in this hypothetical example, the $100,000 life insurance policy is worth approximately $23,000 to the owner.

Of course, this is a theoretical exercise. The costs of selling the policy (e.g., any broker commissions or other fees you may have to pay) are not included -- in a real-life example, those costs must be considered as they will impact the bottom-line cash payment you receive. Also, keep in mind that investors have to consider how much they're willing to pay for your policy in light of the risk they're assuming in taking on the responsibility of paying the premiums on the policy for as long as you live. If the policy stays active beyond the seven years predicted in the example above, the investor will need to pay more premiums than expected and wait for the death benefit to be paid out.

Finally, another important lesson from the illustration of how the price for a life insurance policy is calculated on the secondary market is to understand there is a point at which the policy will have no value. When the combination of premium payments and the investment return of the investor exceeds the payout they will eventually receive from the death benefit, the policy will have a price of zero because it simply will not have enough value to a buyer.

Case Studies

There are numerous sophisticated methods of valuing a life insurance policy in existence today, some of which even use advanced software tools that attempt to predict how much a policy is worth.[46] But the proof is in the pudding, isn't it?

The three examples below are real-life situations illustrating the specifics of life insurance policies that were sold as life settlements. [47] [48] [49]

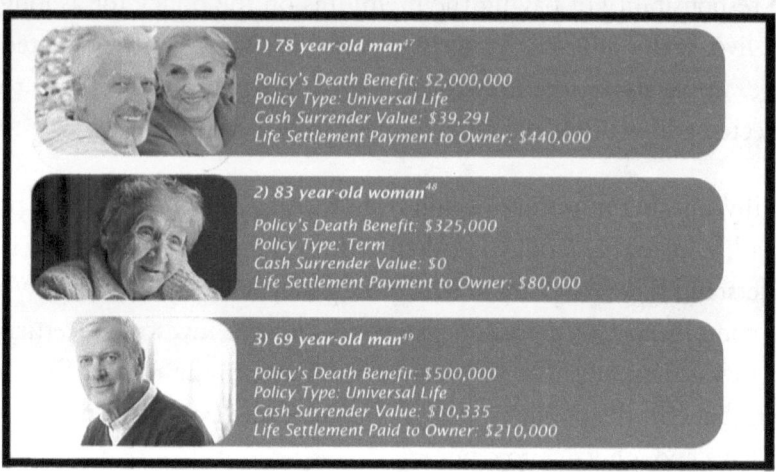

1) 78 year-old man[47]

Policy's Death Benefit: $2,000,000
Policy Type: Universal Life
Cash Surrender Value: $39,291
Life Settlement Payment to Owner: $440,000

2) 83 year-old woman[48]

Policy's Death Benefit: $325,000
Policy Type: Term
Cash Surrender Value: $0
Life Settlement Payment to Owner: $80,000

3) 69 year-old man[49]

Policy's Death Benefit: $500,000
Policy Type: Universal Life
Cash Surrender Value: $10,335
Life Settlement Paid to Owner: $210,000

Remember: You Hold the Cards

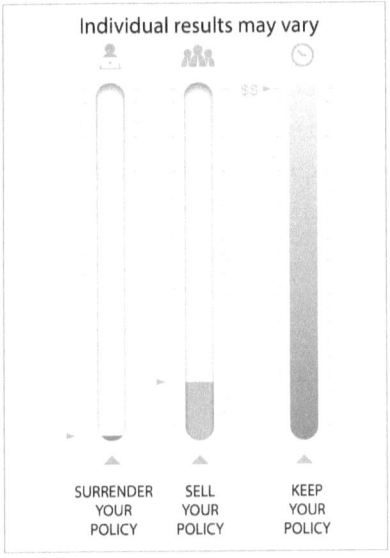

Cash meter example

Individual results may vary

SURRENDER YOUR POLICY   SELL YOUR POLICY   KEEP YOUR POLICY

SOURCE: 2014 LONDON BUSINESS SCHOOL/2010 GAO REPORT ANALYSIS

In trying to understand how much your life insurance policy is worth, please remember that the consumer owns the asset that investors are seeking to purchase -- that means you're holding the cards and you get to decide whether to pursue the transaction or not. To that end, there are a few key things that seniors should bear in mind with respect to the value of a policy.

- Life settlements pay far more than surrender value

As we documented in Chapter Two, when life insurance policy owners enter into life settlements, they realize an average of seven times the amount of the policy's cash surrender value, based on an analysis of a 2010 survey by the U.S. Government Accountability Office. More recently, a 2014 study by the London Business School found that Americans who sold their unwanted life insurance policies collectively received more than four times the amount they would have received had they surrendered them to their life insurance companies.

- Innovative transactions may be possible

There may be some innovative transaction options available for your unique circumstances. For example, perhaps you're struggling to make premium payments on your policy, but you don't want to let the policy lapse because you still need to maintain a death benefit for your loved ones. In this case, you may be able to sell a portion of the policy for an immediate cash payment while still retaining a portion of the death benefit for your beneficiary.[50] There are other creative arrangements that may be possible, you just need to lay out your specific needs and explore the options.

- Seek independent counsel before you decide

If you decide to put your life insurance policy up for sale on the life settlement market, you are still the owner of the policy and you have all of the power in your hands for what to do with that asset. If the potential buyer decides to extend an offer for your policy, you can review that offer with your trusted advisors and determine whether it represents a good deal for you or needs to be raised in order for it to make sense. You may also choose to retain a life settlement broker, who will solicit competing offers from other potential buyers and help you compare the offers so you can choose the best one. Naturally, you're always free to decline all offers and keep your policy for yourself, just like you can with any other form of personal property.

There may not be a printed menu where you can find the exact price that your policy will command in the marketplace, but it's not very complicated to understand the key factors that will influence that price. As with any asset you might want to consider selling for a cash payment, you just need to know a few key pieces of information to determine its worth, then test the market and see how much your policy is worth. It's always a good idea to seek financial and legal advice to help you determine whether you are receiving fair offers.

Chapter Seven

Anatomy of a Life Settlement Transaction

If you have decided that you no longer need or can afford your life insurance policy -- and after exploring your range of options, you have determined that the best option for you is to sell the policy for maximum value through a life settlement -- the next step will be to find the right professionals who can assist you with exploring a possible transaction.

A good starting point for you is to talk to your trusted financial advisors. This may be a financial planner, an investment advisor, an attorney, a bank trust officer and/or perhaps your accountant. These are the folks who know your personal circumstances, your financial objectives and perhaps your family dynamics. They are uniquely qualified to guide your decision making process when it comes to the evaluation of your assets, including your life insurance policy.

The next step will be an important one: you will need to reach out to qualified professionals who are experts in life settlement transactions.

Work with the Right People

As you may recall from Chapter Three, there are two primary groups of professionals involved in making a life settlement transaction happen: (1)

Life settlement brokers, the professionals who "shop" your life insurance policy to potential buyers and represent you in the evaluation of any offers[51]; and (2) Life settlement providers, the professionals who serve as prospective buyers of your policy and will work with you to complete the transaction.[52]

It's entirely up to you as the policy owner to decide whether you wish to work with a life settlement broker to explore the sale of your policy or to work directly with a life settlement provider. Regardless of what you decide, there are some important questions you should ask in order to make sure that you're selecting the right people to help you sell your policy, such as the following[53]:

1) How long has your firm been in the life settlement business, how many professionals does it employ and how many years of experience does its top management have in the business? Is the firm a member in good standing of the Life Insurance Settlement Association (LISA)?

2) Is your firm fully licensed in jurisdictions where it conducts business and has the firm ever been convicted of violating any life settlement regulations in any jurisdictions?

3) Have you or your firm ever been found guilty by any state or federal regulatory agency for violating any life settlement laws and/or regulations? Have you or your firm ever been found guilty of any acts deemed to be a felony?

4) While acting on my behalf, will you provide me with total disclosure of all information and interaction among providers with whom you are negotiating a sale price for my policy?

5) How is your compensation determined, does it come out of the proceeds of selling my policy and who pays it? Likewise, will I

know if there are any other parties to be compensated for selling my policy and how much their compensation will be?

6) Will you keep me informed about the progress of the sales transaction at specific times?

7) Will you provide me with any references to previous clients for whom you have successfully completed transactions?

The authors' website (http://www.insurancehiddenvalue.com) provides more information and access to life settlement professionals who are subject to a set of ethical standards of practice. These professionals have been required to attest on an annual basis they are abiding by all life settlement laws, regulations and ethical requirements.

The Transaction Timeline

Once you have consulted with your trusted financial advisors and have engaged the services of a qualified life settlement professional to assist you with the sale of your policy, you will embark on a seven-step journey in pursuit of a successful transaction.

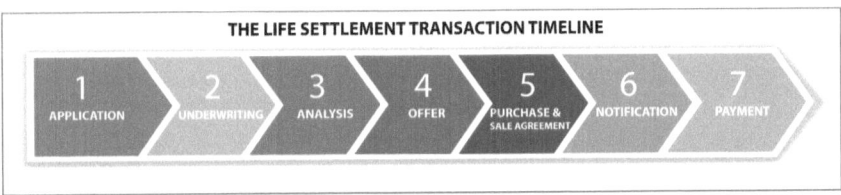

Step 1 | Application

The policy owner fills out an application and provides a copy of the policy, proof of ownership (verification of coverage) and insured information -- including a list of physicians and your medical records. You'll also need to sign a form to comply with the Health Insurance Portability And Accountability Act (HIPAA) and provide an updated policy illustration. It is crucial that you discuss all your privacy and security rights at this time so you understand how your personal information will be reviewed and protected.

Step 2 | Underwriting

The life settlement professional submits your medical records for review by an independent life expectancy company. These professionals provide information about any medical problems you have and calculate the probable life expectancy using actuarial and physician experts.

Step 3 | Analysis

Each life settlement provider calculates what they believe to be the market value for your policy. Companies may consider a number of factors when valuing a policy (although we addressed those primary factors in Chapter Six) so it's possible that different prospective buyers will come up with varying numbers.

Step 4 | Offer

Each provider who is contacted will either decline or extend an offer to the policy owner or broker, if you chose to engage one (a broker will seek competing offers from other providers/buyers). You are absolutely free to accept or decline any offer.

Step 5 | Purchase and Sale Agreement

If you accept an offer, the provider that made the offer will prepare a purchase and sale agreement, as well as other legal documents formalizing the transaction. The policy owner, insured and beneficiaries then sign this package. The provider will do a final review of all the details and countersign the package. At this stage, the funds for the settlement transaction are then placed in an escrow account. You will have a certain number of days to void the transaction, should you find the need to do so.

Step 6 | Notification

The life insurance carrier is notified of the change of policy ownership and beneficiary to the new owner of your policy, the provider whom you chose.

Step 7 | Payment

Upon written verification of the change of ownership and beneficiary, the escrow agent releases the settlement payment. The full payment for your policy is transferred to you all at once and is ready to be deposited into your bank account.

Making the Process Go Easier

Depending on the complexity of your individual situation, a typical life settlement transaction will take between two to four months. Of course, some transactions may be able to be expedited and go faster; others may take longer if there are delays in obtaining medical records, policy statements and other necessary documents.[54]

There are a few simple things that you and your advisors can do to make the process go as easy as possible. For example, it's important to keep making the premium payments on your policy throughout the various stages of the transaction. This is because most insurance carriers will decline to transfer ownership of the policy if your premiums are delinquent. Also, it's a good idea to obtain in advance as many of the "standard" documents you'll need to turn over eventually to a potential buyer -- such as an in-force illustration, a current verification of coverage and your most recent annual statement from the carrier.[55] Having these items in your hands and ready to be turned over to a buyer when the time comes will reduce the risk of problems during the review process and help complete the transaction faster.

Conclusion

Unlocking a Hidden Asset

Mary was a 76 year-old retired school teacher living in New York. She received a Social Security check each month and still had a little money trickling in from a modest pension, but her remaining savings had been reduced by an erratic stock market and a divorce. Mary was forced to live on a strict budget, limited in how much she could afford to do in retirement.

Then one autumn day, Mary's friend invited her to come along on a once-in-a-lifetime trip to Europe the following spring. A group of retired ladies had plans to visit all of the historic sites, inspiring museums, glorious cathedrals, luxurious hotels and breathtaking vineyards located in a dozen countries from England to Greece. Mary pictured herself in the audience for a play in London's West End, wandering the countless rooms of the Louvre in Paris, staring at Michelangelo's masterpiece on the ceiling of the Sistine Chapel in Rome, and dining on tapas at a waterfront restaurant in Barcelona.

These were the experiences she had longed to have for years! Oh sure, she had taken the occasional family vacation when the kids were on school breaks, but this was her time to enjoy all of the sweet pleasures of life without worrying about anyone else's schedule or packing anyone else's luggage.

Just one problem. Where was she going to find the money for airfare, hotels, restaurants, trains, taxis and theaters? Mary's checking account balance was bleak and she just couldn't risk pulling the cash out of her savings account, leaving her with even less of a safety net to come back to, after the trip was a bright memory. As she was about to let her friend know that she'd have to decline the invitation, her phone rang.

"Hi Mom, how'd the doctor visit go?" asked Susie, Mary's daughter.

"Oh it went fine, he said that I just need to keep taking my medicine and try to get a little more exercise," said Mary.

"Sounds like good advice, your grandkids want you around for a long time. Hey by the way, I'm going to forward you an article I read online about something called a life settlement. Not sure if you still have that old life insurance policy, but if so you might want to read this article. It says that you can get immediate cash by selling a life insurance policy that you no longer need or can afford. I figured that Paul and I don't really need the death benefit from your life insurance anymore since we have our own families, so maybe you could just sell the policy and get some cash in your hands that you can use while your health is still holding up."

"Hmm, that's an interesting idea. Thanks Susie, I'll check it out."

Within a matter of days, Mary was speaking to a licensed life settlement professional. The two of them briefly discussed the details of a $200,000 Universal Life policy that had been sitting in Mary's file cabinet for years while she faithfully paid the premiums every June. The professional told Mary that he was confident they would find someone interested in buying the policy, he just needed some more records from her and a few documents.

A couple weeks later, Mary was presented with some attractive offers for her policy and entered into a life settlement transaction. Ten weeks after that, a check for $40,000 was deposited into Mary's checking account. The once-in-a-lifetime adventure vacation in Europe with the ladies was now possible, with plenty of cash to spare!

Finding Value in Life Insurance for Today

Mary's story is not unusual. Each year, thousands of American seniors discover the opportunity to unlock the hidden value of their life insurance policies through life settlement transactions.[56] These are hard-working folks who are able to retire mortgages, pay off unexpected medical bills or take dream vacations with the cash they obtain by selling their policies.

If you think a life settlement may be a good option for you to consider, there are a few places where you can go to obtain more information in figuring out whether the life settlement option is right for you:

The Hidden Value in Your Life Insurance
http://www.insurancehiddenvalue.com

Funds for Your Retirement
http://www.fundsforyourretirement.com

Bayston-Teague Publishing, LLC
http://www.baystonteague.com

Life Insurance Settlement Association
http://www.lisa.org

Insurance Studies Institute
http://www.insurancestudies.org/

LongTermCare.gov
http://longtermcare.gov/costs-how-to-pay/using-life-insurance-to-pay-for-long-term-care/

A Closing Word

The goal of this book was simple: to educate American seniors that their life insurance policies may have economic value to them while they're alive, not just to their beneficiaries when they die. Our focus throughout has been on raising awareness of seniors about the options available to them if they have concluded they no longer need or can afford a life insurance policy, not to encourage anyone to sell a life insurance policy they want to keep for the benefit of their loved ones.

To that end, our journey started with a basic explanation of how a life insurance policy works and a review of the range of options available to policy owners if they no longer need or can afford their policy. Along the way, we explored the history of life settlements and identified the various participants in the American life settlements industry -- including how seniors are now protected by rigorous life settlements regulation -- and explained who purchases life settlements from seniors and why they do it. We tried to lay out who may and who may not be good candidates for life settlements, detailed how the value of a life insurance policy is determined by potential buyers, then concluded the journey by walking through the anatomy of a life settlement transaction.

We have a deep conviction that every single American senior is entitled to know the full range of alternatives that exist to lapsing or surrendering a life insurance policy back to their insurance company. Hopefully, this book has introduced you to one of those options -- the emerging marketplace of life settlements -- and has illustrated that it's a safe, ethical and regulated industry. But only you, with the counsel of your trusted financial advisors and input of your close friends and family members, can determine whether a life settlement makes sense for your unique situation.

Thousands of American seniors have already successfully unlocked the hidden value in their life insurance policies, easing their financial burdens and helping them to truly make the most of their golden years.

References

1   http://laborcenter.berkeley.edu/pdf/2015/RetirementSavingsCrisis.pdf
2   http://healthleadersmedia.com
3   http://money.usnews.com/money/retirement/articles/2015/10/22/
    what-no-social-security-cola-could-mean-for-you
4   http://www.huffingtonpost.com/2014/10/27/die-than-retire-
    poor_n_6042682.html
5   http://www.insuranceblogbychris.com/history-life-insurance/
6   http://www.lifehealthpro.com/2011/09/01/the-origins-of-an-industry
7   https://www.lifehappens.org/industry-resources/2015barometer
8   https://www.acli.com/Tools/Industry%20Facts/Life%20Insurers%20
    Fact%20Book/Pages/RP15-010.aspx
9   http://www.lisa.org/consumer-advisors#tabs00
10 http://goodneighbors.com/post/96357024982/liam1
11 https://bepp.wharton.upenn.edu/files/?whdmsaction=public:main.
    file&fileID=8485
12 http://www.wsj.com/articles/
    cost-of-universal-life-insurance-stings-retirees-1439172119?alg=y
13 http://insurancenewsnet.com/innarticle/2015/11/16/more-life-carriers-raise-
    rates-on-older-blocks-of-business.html
14 http://www.lisa.org/consumer-advisors/advisor-news/2015/10/23/unexpected-
    life-insurance-premium-hikes-pose-major-threat-to-seniors-say-experts-at-
    2015-fall-life-settlement-conference
15 https://www.acli.com/Consumers/Life%20Insurance/Pages/Lapses%20
    and%20Surrenders.aspx
16 http://www.lisa.org/life-policy-owners/consumer-blog/blog/2015/02/25/
    lapsed-life-insurance-policies-an-astounding-number
17 http://www.lifehealthpro.com/2015/10/12/
    the-benefits-of-recommending-the-sale-of-a-clients
18 http://www.insurancestudies.org
19 http://www.lifehealthpro.com/2013/09/16/
    life-settlements-what-you-dont-know-can-hurt-you

20 https://supreme.justia.com/cases/federal/us/222/149/case.html

21 https://scholar.google.com/scholar_case?case=9405495298337520720&q=
    grigsby+v.+russell&hl=en&as_sdt=2006&as_vis=1

22 https://books.google.com/books?id=tay74Q1ZbpQC&pg=PT26&lpg=
    PT26&dq=hipaa+transfer+life+insurance+ownership&source=bl&ots=
    eC4yh8hfHF&sig=HSb438HoEzzCKu8iohCLIcrWFyI&hl=en&sa=X&ved=
    0ahUKEwi0_8yg7b7JAhUF4SYKHZkpDHIQ6AEILzAH#v=onepage&q=
    hipaa%20transfer%20life%20insurance%20ownership&f=false

23 http://www.naic.org/store/free/MDL-697.pdf

24 http://ifawebnews.com/2009/06/26/seniors-unaware-of-life-settlement-option-
    study-says/?mobile_switch=mobile

25 https://govt.westlaw.com/calregs/Browse/Home/California/CaliforniaCodeof
    Regulations?guid=I6A65FAA14DF511E18528DD9D68D34030&origination
    Context=documenttoc&transitionType=Default&contextData=(sc.Default)

26 http://www.sec.gov/investor/alerts/lifesettlements-bulletin.htm

27 http://www.lisa.org/industry-resources/life-settlement-industry-timeline

28 https://www.conning.com/pressrelease-detail.aspx?id=11185

29 http://www.lifehealthpro.com/2013/06/25/7-positive-trends-for-life-
    settlements

30 https://eapps.naic.org/cis/

31 http://www.lisa.org/consumer-advisors/helping-clients/Determine-if-a-life-
    settlement-is-the-right-solution

32 http://www.insure.com/life-settlements/life-settlements-industry-tries-new-
    spin.html

33 https://www.conning.com/pressrelease-detail.aspx?id=12916

34 http://partners4prosperity.com/life-settlement-investments-pros-and-cons-
    facts-faqs

35 http://www.coventry.com/assets/Marketing_Tools_Pdfs/LifeSettlements
    Study_LBS.pdf

36 http://www.finalternatives.com/node/30404

37 http://www.ubsnet.com/assets/Uploads/Newspdf/Mobile-News/Banner-COI-
    Increase-7-22-15.pdf

38 http://www.lifehealthpro.com/2015/06/15/dont-get-confused-life-settlement-
    transactions-are?t=life-settlements

39 http://www.lisa.org/about/policy-statement-fractionalized-interests

40 http://www.newretirement.com/Services/Life-Settlement-Eligible.aspx

41 https://www.irs.gov/pub/irs-drop/rr-09-13.pdf

42 http://www.bna.com/application-of-life-settlements/

43 http://www.investmentnews.com/article/20131216/FREE/131219929/
    resurgence-ahead-for-life-settlements-industry

44 http://www.thelifeline.com/sites/default/files/
    FINAL_LifeSettlements-WP_Wealthmgmt_2.6_15.pdf

45 http://insurancestudies.org/wp-content/uploads/2010/05/ISI_2008_LS_
    Pricing_Methodologies_Full.pdf

46 http://lewisellis.com/specialties/software-solutions/le-settleware-life-
    settlement-pricing-tool

47 https://www.welcomefunds.com/casestudies.php

48 http://www.lisettlements.com/previous-case-studies/

49 http://atinafunding.com/life-settlement-case-studies-2/

50 http://www.lifehealthpro.com/2014/11/21/retained-death-benefit-life-
    settlements-considerin

51 http://www.mass.gov/ocabr/docs/doi/producer/applications/life-settlement-
    broker-corporate-requirements.pdf

52 http://www.insurance.ca.gov/0200-industry/0050-renew-license/0200-
    requirements/LifeSettlementProvid.cfm

53 http://www.lisa.org/consumer-advisors/helping-clients/identifying-a-life-
    settlement-firm

54 https://www.welcomefunds.com/life-settlement-consumer-education.html

55 http://www.lifehealthpro.
    com/2013/02/26/4-ways-to-smooth-the-life-settlement-process

56 http://insurancenewsnet.com/innarticle/2015/06/22/the-new-face-of-life-
    settlements.html

www.ingramcontent.com/pod-product-compliance
Lightning Source LLC
Chambersburg PA
CBHW021906170526
45157CB00005B/1994